day by day guidance

Paul E. Little, who died in a car crash in 1975, was well known for his travelling and teaching ministry. He was an associate professor of evangelism at Trinity Evangelical Divinity School, Deerfield, Illinois, USA, and assistant to the president of the Inter-Varsity Christian Fellowship of America. He was closely involved in the Lausanne Conference on Evangelism in 1974

day by day guidance

PAUL LITTLE

FALCON

London FALCON

A FALCON BOOKLET

published by
Church Pastoral Aid Society
Falcon Court, 32 Fleet Street, London, EC4Y 1DB

distributed overseas by
Australia: EMU Book Agencies Ltd, 63 Berry Street, Granville, 2142, NSW
New Zealand: Scripture Union Bookshop, PO Box 760, Wellington

day by day guidance

ISBN 0 85491 139 1
Originally published in the United States (IVCS) 1971
First published in the United Kingdom (CPAS) 1976
Text © Paul E. Little 1971, Marie E. Little 1975
Biblical quotations are from Today's English Version, except where otherwise stated

DESIGNED AND PRODUCED IN THE UNITED KINGDOM
Photoset in Optima type by
Keyspools Ltd, Golborne, Lancashire
Printed offset litho and bound by
Stanley L. Hunt (Printers) Ltd, Rushden, Northamptonshire

contents

	page
Introductory	7
Two aspects of God's will	8
Prerequisites for special guidance	10
Principles of guidance	14
Common mistakes to avoid	18
God's will for me	24

Teach me thy way, O Lord . . .

Suppose, for a moment, that the Lord Jesus Christ were to grant you the answer to one question—any question you wanted to ask. What would that question be?

My guess is that it would probably relate in some way to knowing God's will for your life. After all, to a committed Christian this is really the only thing that counts. Our peace and satisfaction depend on knowing that God is guiding us. And the absence of that certainty leaves us fearful and restless.

But we have a problem because we are confused about what the will of God is in the first place. And unless we are clear about that, we really cannot make much progress. Most people speak of God's will as something you have or don't have. 'Have you discovered God's will for your life?' they ask each other. What they usually mean is, 'Have you discovered God's *blueprint* for your life?' But the fact is that God seldom reveals an entire blueprint. So if you are looking for that blueprint in its entirety, you are likely to be disappointed. What God does most frequently reveal, however, is the next step in his will. But this leads us into the fuller question of what exactly God's will is.

It is important to understand at the outset that God has a plan and purpose for your life. This is one of the sensational aspects of being a Christian—to know that your life can be tied into God's plan and purpose not only for time but for eternity. Paul writes, 'God is our Maker, and in our union with Christ Jesus he has created us for a life of good works, which he has already prepared for us to do' (Ephesians 2:10). David, in Psalm 37:23, says, 'The Lord guides a man safely in the way he should go and is pleased with his conduct'. And in Acts 13:2 we read: 'While they were serving the Lord and fasting, the Holy Spirit said to them, "Set apart for me Barnabas and Saul, to do the work to which I have called them".'

8 *Day by Day Guidance*

Not only does God have a plan for us, but he has promised to reveal it to us. In Psalm 73:24, David says of God, 'You guide me with your advice, and at the end you will receive me with honour'. In Psalm 32:8, God promises, 'I will teach you the way you should go; I will instruct you and advise you.'

Finally, those classic verses, Proverbs 3:5–6, two of the most compact verses on guidance in the whole Bible, say, 'Trust in the Lord with all your heart. Never rely on what you think you know. Remember the Lord in everything you do, and he will show you the right way.'

TWO ASPECTS OF GOD'S WILL

There are two aspects to God's will. The first is that aspect of his will and his plan which has already been revealed in his word and which applies to every Christian. The second aspect involves those decisions in which God has given no specific instructions.

Has it ever struck you that the vast majority of the will of God for your life has already been revealed in the Bible? That is a crucial thing to grasp.

There are many positive commands. For instance, we are commanded by our Lord to go to all peoples everywhere and make them disciples. We know it is the will of God (from Romans 8:29) that we are to become like Christ. If you want more details, read the book of James, list all the specific commands there, and you will have a good start on the will of God for your life.

Scripture also contains many negative commands. God tells us in unmistakable terms in 2 Corinthians 6:14 that we are not to 'try to work together as equals with unbelievers.' This means, among other things, that a Christian is never to marry an unbeliever. Are any of you praying for guidance about whether you should marry a non-Christian? Save your breath.

The late A. W. Tozer pointed out that we should

Day by Day Guidance 9

never seek guidance on what God has already forbidden. Nor should we ever seek guidance in the areas where he has already said Yes and given us a command. Then, Tozer suggests, in most other things God has no preference.

God really does not have a great preference whether you eat steak or chicken. He is not desperately concerned about whether you wear a green shirt or a blue shirt. In many areas of life, God invites us to consult our own sanctified preferences. When we are pleased, God is pleased. That is a wonderful thing to know, isn't it?

Then Tozer points out that there are, on the other hand, areas in which we need special guidance. These are the areas of life where there is no specific statement like, 'Thou, John Jones, shalt be an engineer in Birmingham'; or, 'Thou, Mary Smith, shalt marry Fred Bloggs.' No verse in the Bible will give you that kind of detail in your life. But God has promised us special guidance in these areas. The Lord spoke to the prophet Isaiah, 'I am the Lord your God, who teaches you to profit, who leads you in the way you should go' (48:17 RSV).

By recognizing the two aspects of God's will—namely, what is already specifically revealed in his word and what is not—we get away from the static concept of the blueprint. The will of God is not like a magic package let down out of heaven by a string, a package we grope after in desperation and hope sometime in the future to clasp to our hearts.

The will of God is far more like a scroll that unrolls every day. In other words, God has a will for you and me today and tomorrow and the next day and the day after that. Now it may well be that a decision we make this week or next week will commit us for three months, or two years, or five or ten years, or for a lifetime. But the fact still remains that the will of God is something to be discerned and to be lived out each day of our lives. It is not something to be grasped as a package once for all. Our call, therefore, is basically not to follow a plan or a blueprint, or to go to a place or take up a work, but rather to follow the Lord Jesus Christ. When we realize this, then we will begin to sense something of its dynamic.

PREREQUISITES FOR SPECIAL GUIDANCE

Now, after understanding something of the two aspects of the will of God, we need to look at the prerequisites for knowing the will of God in the unspecified areas of our lives.

● One prerequisite is *to be a child of God*.

One day some people asked Jesus directly, 'What can we do in order to do God's works?' And Jesus answered specifically and clearly, 'This is the work God wants you to do: believe in the one he sent' (John 6:29). We must first come to Jesus in a commitment of faith to him as Saviour and Lord. Then we are God's children and can be guided by him as our Father. The Lord said in John 10:3, 'The sheep hear his voice as he calls his own sheep by name, and he leads them out'.

● The second prerequisite is *to obey, at least in the desire of our hearts, the will of God in those areas where we know what it is*.

What is the point of God's guiding us in areas in which he has not been specific when we are apparently unconcerned about areas in which he is specific? Mark Twain once wryly observed, 'It's not the parts of the Bible I don't understand that bother me, it's the parts I do understand.' Perhaps this is the problem for some of us now. We need to begin to obey in those specific areas.

We know, for example, that we ought to be meeting with the Lord every day in prayer. 'But,' you say, 'you don't know how busy I am. I have to do this . . . and that . . . and the other. . . .' All of us have 24 hours equally. It is merely a matter of setting priorities. If you are going to meet with God every day, it means you decide when you are going to bed, when you will get up and what you are going to study.

You may have vaguely wanted to witness to that friend in the same office, or the woman you meet in the supermarket every week. Then decide when you are going to do it. Attempt to contact that friend to see if there is any openness to the gospel.

What are the areas of the will of God that you already understand? To what extent are you acting on that understanding?

● The third prerequisite, and I think the most crucial, is *to be willing to accept the will of God in these unspecified areas of our lives before knowing what it is.*

In other words, we must accept God's will in advance. For most of us, I suspect, this is where the real problem lies. If we are really honest, we would have to admit that our attitude is, 'Lord, show me what your will is so that I can decide whether it fits in with what I have in mind.' In essence we are saying, 'Just lift the curtain a minute and let me see so that I can decide whether I want to do it or not. Show me whether I'm to be married or not. Show me where in the world you want me to be and what you want me to do. If it's the Bahamas or the Costa Brava or some wonderful place like that, then maybe I'll consider it a little more seriously.'

If we stopped to analyse this attitude, we should be shocked, for what we are doing is insulting God. We are saying, 'I think I know better than you, God, what will make me happy. I don't trust you. If I let you run my life, you're going to shortchange me.' Have you ever felt that? It is a solemn thing to realize.

We have the tragic, mistaken idea that we must choose between doing what we want to do and being happy, and doing what God wants us to do and being miserable. We think that the will of God is some horrible thing which he shoves under our nose and demands, 'All right! Are you willing, are you willing?' If we could just get out from under his clammy hands, we could really swing.

Nothing could be further from the truth. Such notions are a slur on the character of God. So many of us see God as a kind of celestial Scrooge who peers over the balcony of heaven trying to find anybody who is enjoying life. And when he spots a happy person, he yells, 'Now cut that out!' That concept of God should make us shudder because it's blasphemous!

We need to have the tremendous truth of Romans 8:32 deeply planted in our hearts: 'He did not even keep back his own Son, but offered him for us all! He gave us his Son—will he not freely give us all things?' If you can get hold of that verse, memorize it, meditate on it and allow it to get hold of you, you will have solved 90% of your problem with desire for the will of God, because you will realize the God who loved us enough to die for us when we did not care that much for him is not going to shortchange us in life when we give our lives to him. As someone has put it, 'Having given us the package, do you think God will deny us the ribbon?'

Think of it in human terms for the moment. I have two children, a girl Debbie and a son Paul. When my children come to me and say, 'Daddy, I love you,' do you think I respond by saying, 'Ah, children, that's just what I've been waiting to hear. Into that cupboard for three weeks. Bread and water. I've just been waiting for you to tell me you love me so I can make your life miserable!' Of course not. They could get anything they wanted out of me at that point.

Day by Day Guidance

Do you think that God is any less loving than a human father? God's love far transcends any love that we as humans express. The Bible is constantly drawing contrasts between human love and activity, and our heavenly Father's love. 'As bad as you are,' Jesus says in Luke 11:13, 'you know how to give good things to your children. How much more, then, the Father in heaven will give the Holy Spirit to those who ask him!'

When we come to God and say, 'I love you, and I'm prepared to do your will whatever you want me to do', we can be sure that God is not going to make us miserable. Rather he rejoices and fits our lives into his pattern for us, into that place where he, in his omniscience and love, knows we will fit hand in glove. The one who is our Creator, who made us, who knows us better than we will ever know ourselves, is the one we are talking to. He knows the end from the beginning.

I love the third verse of the hymn, *Still will we trust;*

> Choose for us, God, nor let our weak preferring
> Cheat us of good Thou hast for us designed:
> Choose for us, God; Thy wisdom is unerring.
> And we are fools and blind.

God's will is not loathsome. It is the greatest thing in all of life to get hold of. There is no greater joy or satisfaction than to be in the centre of the will of God and to know it.

In the light of the character of God and considering the experience of people who have known him, I dislike intensely the phrase, 'surrender to the will of God.' To me, that implies kicking, struggling, screaming. It is like saying, 'There is no other way out. I'm running, but I'm caught. I've got to collapse and surrender. It's all over. I give up.'

I far prefer the term, 'affirm the will of God.' If we had any sense at all, every one of us would affirm God's will with confidence and with joy and with deep satisfaction.

This third prerequisite is therefore crucial. It involves eliminating any holdout areas in your life—a relationship, an ambition, a qualification. No more saying, 'I'll go anywhere, Lord, but . . .' or 'I'll go and do anything, but it's got to be with so-and-so.' Rather we will say, 'Lord, you've created me and I belong to you. Even when I was a rebel against you, you loved me enough to die for me. Everything I am and have belongs to you. I'm not my own, I'm bought with a price—the precious blood of Christ—and I consciously and joyfully commit myself to you. Do with me as you choose.' And when we come to that place, we will be able to say with Paul, and mean it in the depths of our hearts, 'What is life? To me, it is Christ!'

We must first, then, understand what the will of God is. Then we must be prepared to accept the prerequisites for knowing it in those areas about which the Bible is not specific. And in the third place we need to understand how, in fact, God guides in the areas in which he has not been specific.

PRINCIPLES OF GUIDANCE

● First, in addition to specific commands, *there are principles in the Word of God which may have direct implications for our situation*.

Several years ago I knew a girl who had signed a contract to teach. In August, she received another offer from a school closer to where she wanted to live. So she broke the original contract. Had she acted on the biblical principle in Psalm 15:4, where God says that he is pleased with a person who 'always does what he promises, no matter how much it may cost him', she would not have done that. The department chairman who told me about the Christian girl's action said her justification was, 'I have a peace about it,' and he commented rather sardonically, 'Isn't that lovely. She's got the peace and I've got the pieces.' I believe that girl missed the will of God. She violated a principle which, if she had been alert and had applied it to her situation, would have given her clear guidance in this specific detail of her life. God guides, then, through his word and its principles.

● Second, *God guides us in prayer as we ask him to show us his will.*

At a conference I went to as a student, one of the speakers asked, 'How many of you who are concerned about the will of God spend five minutes a day asking him to show you his will?' It was as if someone had grabbed me by the throat. At that time I was concerned about what I should do when I graduated. I was running around—going to this meeting, reading that book, trying to find somebody's little formula, 1, 2, 3, 4 and a bell rings—and I was frustrated out of my mind trying to figure out the will of God. I was doing everything but getting into the presence of God and asking him to show me.

Let me ask you the same question: Do you spend even five minutes a day specifically asking God to show you?

As we pray, God often gives us a conviction by the Holy Spirit which deepens, despite new information, to an increasing sense of rightness or oughtness about a course of action. This is quite different from the 'gung ho' emotion which prods us today to get on a plane to Hong Kong, and tomorrow to move to Scotland, and the next day to paddle a canoe up the Amazon, and each day after to go in a different direction. When the Holy Spirit begins to move in our hearts, one conviction deepens and, while we recognize other situations, we sense that this is the will of God for us.

Day by Day Guidance

● Third, *God guides and directs us through circumstances.*

Here, however, we must be particularly on guard. Most of us tend to make circumstances 99% of the guidance. But they are only one of the factors in guidance. Furthermore, we must view circumstances from God's perspective and values; they may be more of a guide negatively than positively.

For instance, if you think that God is leading you to become an engineering apprentice, but you cannot get a job, it may be fairly clear that God does not want you to do that after all. On the other hand, the fact that you are offered three jobs does not necessarily mean that God wants you in engineering. There are other factors to consider.

You may graduate from university and have offers of 15 jobs, but that does not necessarily mean that God wants you to accept any of them. He may have a prior claim on your life that will involve your going into a far corner of the earth. You may even be called of God to do something that the average non-Christian, who sees nothing but the visible world bounded by the cradle and the grave, would consider a tragic waste of time and talent.

Although circumstances, in themselves, are not a guide, God may use them. A summer trip abroad may show you whether and where God wants you to go overseas. In this jet age young people can spend a year, or a summer holiday, in some other culture without too much difficulty. On the other hand, as a result of study and circumstances God might confirm a call to you here in Britain.

Familiarize youself with the needs of the world. While it is quite true that in itself a need is not a call, the overwhelming needs everywhere cannot be ignored. The old illustration of a log carried by nine men on one

Day by Day Guidance

end and three women on the other may be trite and corny, but it has a profound point: which end of the log will you help carry? It is a fact that 90% of full-time Christian workers are in parts of the world which have 10% of the world's population; 10% of them are in population centres comprising 90% of the world's population. Surely this is not the will of God, since he has already told us in his word that he wants every person to hear the gospel. Millions of people have never heard it.

David Howard asks, 'Why should anyone seek more specific direction to serve the Lord overseas than he does to serve in any other capacity or location? It may well be that we should make every effort to go overseas unless God clearly calls us to stay home, rather than the reverse. And as you make the effort, as you begin to move, God will guide. God can close doors very easily. But, as the old saying goes, you can't steer a parked car; you can't pilot a moored ship.'

God will also guide you through circumstances as you get involved in evangelism where you are. It is foolish to think of travelling to some other part of the world if God isn't already using you in the lives of people around you now.

Trust God to give you a solid friendship with at least one person from overseas. Ask God to enable you to share the greatest thing in all of life—the love of Jesus—and to articulate the gospel to your friends. If you are able to get through to both British and overseas students in your college, or to neighbours of all races in your street, God may then put a fire in your bones that will move you to some other part of the world

● Fourth, *God guides us through the counsel of other Christians who are fully committed to the will of God and who know us well*.

This is one of the most neglected dimensions of guidance today. It sounds terribly spiritual to say, 'God led me,' but I am always suspicious of a person who implies that he has a *personal* pipeline to God. When no one else senses that what the person suggests is the will of God, then we had better be careful. God has been blamed for the most outlandish things by people who have confused their own inverted pride with God's will.

Occasionally I hear of a man who, in the name of spiritual guidance, rushes up to a girl and says, 'Sue, God has told me you're to marry me'. I have news for him. If that is the will of God, then Sue is going to get the message too. If she doesn't, someone's radar is jammed, and it's not hard to tell whose.

Are you wondering about marriage, or about whether God might use you in an overseas situation or in the ministry? Talk to some of your mature Christian friends, your ministers, elders in your church and others who know you and are themselves concerned for the will of God. Their counsel may be invaluable. It is true that sometimes we get mixed advice from Christian friends, but their counsel is frequently helpful. Remember what Acts 15 records: 'The Holy Spirit and we have agreed. . . .' I believe God usually guides in that way—a personal conviction corroborated by friends' opinions. Don't be afraid to talk to people whom you think might give you advice you don't want to hear. You may be too emotionally involved in a situation to see it objectively and need somebody to talk straight to you so that you can be realistic in your assessment.

When all four of these factors—the word of God, conviction that he gives us in prayer, circumstances and the counsel of mature Christian friends—converge, it is usually a sign that God is leading and guiding us.

COMMON MISTAKES TO AVOID
Finally I want to discuss some serious mistakes to avoid in thinking about the will of God.

● First, *we must not think that because we want to do something, it can't possibly be God's will.*

That attitude displays a distorted concept of the character of God. We really think he is a celestial killjoy. We need to recognize the wonderful truth of Psalm 37:4: 'Seek your happiness with the Lord, and he will give you what you most desire.' This does not mean, 'Seek your happiness with the Lord, and he will give you an E-type, a Bentley, ten lines in *Who's Who*, and everything else you want'. What it means is that as we seek our happiness with the Lord, our will and God's will begin to coincide. The greatest joy in all of our lives is to do what the Lord wants us to do and to know we are doing it. Then we can say with our Lord, 'My food is to obey the will of him who sent me and finish the work he gave me to do' (John 4:34). Admittedly, we must constantly guard against self-deception, but when we really want to do the will of God, and do it, we have deep joy and satisfaction.

● Second, *we must not feel that every decision we make must have a subjective confirmation.*

I have known people who have been paralyzed and couldn't act at all because they did not have some kind of electrifying liver-shiver about the whole thing. If you are facing an important decision in which God has not given you specific guidance, postpone the decision, if you can, until the way seems clear. But if you must decide by next Saturday, and next Saturday comes and you still don't have clear guidance, then you must trust that God will guide you in the decision. After assessing all the factors, launch out in faith, saying, 'Lord, as I see it, there are four equally valid possibilities in front of me. I see no particular advantage or disadvantage in any of these options. So I am going to go down this third road unless you close the door. I am trusting that you won't let me make a crucial mistake.'

If we do that, we can act joyfully, believing God has guided us. We don't have to spend the next 24 years tormenting ourselves as to whether or not we are in the will of God. God does not play the game of mousetrap with us. He doesn't say, 'Ha, ha. You thought that was the right lane, but it wasn't. Return to Go. Better luck next time.' We must get rid of these distorted concepts of God's character. The God who loved us enough to die for us is not going to play games with our lives. We mean too much to him. Rather, we can claim his promise, 'Trust in the Lord with all your heart. Never rely on what you think you know. Remember the Lord in everything you do, and he will show you the right way.'

● Third, *we must realize that there are often logical implications involved in the will of God.*

If some things are the will of God, then a whole series of other things are automatically the will of God, and we do not have to pray about them. For example, if God leads you to get married, you do not have to spend hours in prayer agonizing over whether or not it is the will of God that you should support your wife. This is painfully self-evident, and yet I have met so many people who do not seem to have grasped it. I once lent a man five pounds, and he is still praying about whether he ought to pay me back.

● Fourth, *we must not think that God's will is necessarily something wild and bizarre.*

Many people are afraid of using their reason in determining God's will. But we must recognize that God is not the author of confusion. When the Scripture says, 'Never rely on what you think you know', it does not mean you have to kiss your brains goodbye. Rather, the Holy Spirit illumines us and then guides our enlightened reason. It may be that he will lead us to do something that is contrary to our unenlightened reason, but the idea that his will is frequently bizarre is very dangerous.

Day by Day Guidance   21

● Fifth, *we must guard carefully against the subtle temptation to what what we are going to do for God.*

This mistake is really critical. There is a vast difference between saying, 'Lord, I'm going to be a businessman (or missionary or whatever) for you,' and asking, 'Lord, what will you have me to do?' It sounds very spiritual to say, 'I'm going to be a businessman for the Lord and make money and give it to the Lord's work.' Or, 'I'll be a missionary for the Lord.' But the Lord has not asked you to decide what you are going to be. He has invited you to recruit and say to the Commander-in-Chief, 'Here I am. Where in the battle line do you want me?'

In this connection, be careful you are not tied too closely to your background so that you think God can use you only in the context of the training you have. God may, and probably will, lead you in the area of your training, but God wants you more than your training. I did my training in accounting and business administration, but God never led me into that field. I have been in student work all the time.

● Sixth, *we must guard against the temptation to take Bible verses out of context to get God's will.*

Some people treat the Bible as a book of magic. You have probably heard of the fellow who opened the Bible and put his finger down on the phrase, 'Judas went out and hanged himself.' That did not comfort him very much, so he tried again. And his finger fell on the verse, 'Go thou and do likewise.' That shook him terribly, so he tried it once more, and the verse he hit on was, 'And what thou doest, do quickly.'

On rare occasions, God will take a verse which has no specific application to you and give you a message through it, but this is the exception rather than the rule. The basic biblical principle is to interpret and understand the Bible in context. When this is violated, God gets blamed for all kinds of things which are merely

22 Day by Day Guidance

human stupidity. I remember a girl a few years ago who was sure God was going to give her a visa for the States because a Bible verse (Isaiah 41:2) said something about God raising up a righteous man from the east. I asked her, 'What about the rest of the verse that says God is going to use him to destroy people with the sword?' She didn't get a visa. God didn't fail. She did—by violating the principle of interpreting Scripture on context.

●Seventh, *we must avoid the mistake of thinking that we can be sure we are in the will of God if everything is moonlight and roses, if we have no problems or stress.*

Frequently, just when we take a step of obedience, the bottom falls out of everything. Then only the confidence that we are in the will of God keeps us going.

Never forget the incident recorded in Mark 4. The disciples, at the Lord's specific command, had got into a boat to head across the Sea of Galilee. After they took this step in obedience to the Lord, the storm broke loose and they thought they were going to lose their lives. But Jesus said to them, 'Why are you frightened? Are you still without faith?'

In Mark 5, Jairus came to our Lord saying, 'My daughter's sick. Will you come and heal her?' The Lord said he would, and Jairus's spirits soared. But on the way a lady who had had a medical problem for 12 years, and who surely could have waited another two hours, interrupted them, and Jesus became involved with her. Jairus's servants came and said, 'Look, don't bother him any longer. Your daughter has died.' Jairus, who had done what was right—had got the answer from the Lord, had followed his will and obeyed—must have been crushed in bitter despair. But our Lord's words to him come to us as well in similar circumstances: 'Do not fear. Only believe.' The test of whether you are in the will of God is not how rosy your circumstances are, but whether you are obeying him.

Day by Day Guidance 23

● **Eighth,** *we must avoid the mistake of thinking that a call to world evangelism or missionary service is any different from a call to anything else.*

Dr Norton Sterrett points out that every Christian—whether a wife, an electrician, a lawyer, a teacher or a cabinet maker—has both the privilege and responsibility to know that he is called by God. And he also has the privilege and responsibility to know whether he is to serve in Cairo or Cardiff. You don't get three more spiritual points in God's book for going overseas rather than staying in Britain, for being 'in the ministry' rather than in some other form of endeavour. We have a false hierarchy of spiritual values which is not biblical at all. Some people overseas ought to be at home, and many people at home ought to be overseas.

The crucial question each of us must ask himself is, 'Am I in the will of God and sure of it?' It is not a question of fastening our spiritual seat belts and hoping we will not be swept by some emotion out of our seats into overseas service. Each of us has the privilege of discovering what God wants us to do.

● Finally I want to suggest that *each of us should avoid the mistake of thinking that if we have ever knowingly and deliberately disobeyed the Lord, we are forever thrown on the scrap heap, can never do the Lord's will and are doomed to 'second best.'*

God has the most wonderful ways of reweaving the strands of our lives. He takes us where we are when we come to him in confession and repentance, and uses us fully again. Our disobedience did not take him by surprise, and his grace reaches right to us.

John Mark is a good example. He seemed to have ruined it all when he started out on the missionary trip with Paul: at the first stop he left and headed back for Jerusalem. You will remember that Paul and Barnabas had such a tussle over whether John Mark should go with them again on the next trip that Paul and Barnabas separated. But it seems that Mark was redeemed by God and redeemed himself, and later had a full and fruitful ministry which Paul commended.

When you are feeling bad, and know you have sinned and ruined it all, remember Peter, too. He denied the Lord. But our Lord took hold of him, restored him and made him a great apostle who has given us a part of the word of God.

GOD'S WILL FOR ME

What is God's will for you? Realize, first, that God's will in most of its aspects is already fully revealed. Be sure you are familiar with it in the word of God. In those areas about which he has not been specific, be assured God will guide you through his word and its principles, as you seek his face in prayer, as you view the circumstances from his point of view, and seek the counsel of other Christians. Then, when you can say, 'Lord, I want to do your will more than anything else in life,' and as you avoid some of the mistakes which are often based on a distortion of the character of God, you will know where in the world and how in the world God wants you to serve him. He will show you what his will for you is today, and the next day, and the day after that.

Have you ever affirmed the will of God in your life personally? Paul, in Romans 12, invites you: 'So then, my brothers, because of God's many mercies to us, I make this appeal to you: offer yourselves as a living sacrifice to God, dedicated to his service and pleasing to him. This is the true worship that you should offer. Do not conform outwardly to the standards of this world, but let God transform you inwardly by a complete change of your mind. Then you will be able to know the will of God—what is good, and is pleasing to him, and is perfect.'